Heart Poems

by

Robert Eaton Sokol

Copyright © 2019 by Robert Eaton Sokol

ISBN-13: 978-1-61957-007-8
ISBN-10: 1-61957-007-6

BISAC: Language Arts & Disciplines

/Poetry All rights reserved.

No part of this book may be reproduced or transmitted in any form or by any means, electronic or mechanical, including photocopying, recording, or by any information storage and retrieval system, without permission in writing from the copyright owner.

This book was printed in the United States of America.

Okab Publishing, LLC
P.O. Box 79029
Charlotte, NC 28271

Dedication

I dedicate this and all my writings to:

My parents, Oscar and Frances Sokol, who hired a tutor when I was 16. I could not read well and had very poor reading comprehension. I had almost no recollection of anything I did read. She taught me words and word meanings so at least I could start. They then sent me to a special school so I could learn. My high school English Teacher, Mrs. Martha Crowley, taught me how to focus because my eyes fluttered when I attempted to focus. She had an amazing speed-reading machine that did this. I was not dumb and trying harder was not my problem. I simply could not "see word order."

My beloved wife, Dorothy, who constantly encourages me to write even more, to expand my already expansive imagination to greater heights. I am a Heart Poet. I write from my Heart perspective first, then my mind. If I do not feel it, I do not write it. But when I do, words flow effortlessly and with love.

Preface

Poetry is a suggestive art Using symbols and direct imitation of Life, it stimulates the imagination of the reader through imagery, taking strong hold of their feelings, arousing them to passionate reaction. It also appeals to understanding, and is, therefore, capable of directing lessons of wisdom.

Poetry is the spontaneous overflow of powerful feelings, recollected in tranquility. It reflects the beauty of thought, of feeling, of expression and technical skill. It should be an outlet for one's own unspoken thoughts and varied moods. It makes articulate, our inadequate speech giving adequate expression to our static, yet kinetic loves, joys, glories, furnishing release and relief of one's fears, grief and sorrows.

A poet's job is to salute the mind by creating imagery through the senses; the nose, the ears, sight, touch and taste, creating memories of moments past and views of the present. It is this task, recounting for our senses and experiences, without doubt and in as few words as possible that accurately describe the experience and/ or view of life.

Table of Contents

A Father's Love	1
A Trickle	2
Ah So	3
Air Paddles Huming	4
All Mine, This Paint Brush	5
All Yours, This Birthday	6
Already Imagined	7
Anticipation: My Heart is Burning, Churning	8
Appreciation	9
Arrogance	10
Autumn is Here	11
Being in Love with Me	12
Blindness: Keeping it Real.	14
Breakfast and So On…	15
Butterflys and Loose Skies	16
Close Your Eyes	17
Come Pray with Me	18
Courage	19
Cracked Illusion	20
Day and Night, Baby	21
Disarming Farming and Dangerous Work	22
It's Chilly Outside Summer's Gone!	23
Fathers Seeking Sunshine	24
Fear and Discovery	25
Finding Courage	26
Fireplace	27
Good By, For Now.	28
House Broken	29
I Am	30
I am Right Here, Before the Day	31
I Am There	32

I Choose Life	35
I Know You, Father	36
I Wish Upon You	37
Imagination, Notion of Fancy	38
Joy and Fear	39
Killer of the Crumbs	40
Kiss Me	41
Little and Naughty	42
Love and God	43
Love Song to Him	44
Me	45
Mom Said, "Remember,	46
Moon Shining	47
Morning Hug, Bugging Me	48
My Heart Rate	49
Oh, The Suckers,	50
On Darkned Confusion	51
Please Repeat the Words	52
Reddened Tear Drops	53
Remembering Fathers	54
So Rare	56
Somber is A Phonomenom, A Mood: A Sparrow Sailing Through Shallows.	57
Sometimes You Have to Ask Them to Leave, Not Too Politely.	58
Stormy Weather, Kissing Me Softly.	59
Sunlight and Billowy Clouds	60
The Beat Goes On---Pure Joy	61
The Divide: Let's Talk (Not Balk)	62
The never-ending story, A salute to courage	63
The Storm (Is Here) Arrived	64
There Is No Limit To God's Love	65
This Slippery Slope	66
This Time, It's Sublime	67
Time Stands For No One	68

Took Me From Down Seed	69
Toy Store and More Suckers.	70
Wandering Home at Night was Tight.	72
What's Here, This Time?	73
What Poetry Does For and to Me	74
About the Author	75

A Father's Love

By RobertEatonSokol

All I expect,
I expect of me.
All I anticipate,
Comes from my heart.
All I love,
I love intentionally.
All my kindness comes from
My rejection of fear.
I am a seed of rich living,
Fueled by my Joy.

To my Dear, Loving Sons.
And so it is.
Dad

A Trickle
By RobertEatonSokol

Dicey water tickles
Icy rocks (cleansing) trickling
Pebbles below slowly,
Leveling in pools where schools
of Baby fish feed off this dish of
Delish gifts of beads of seeds of knats swarming.

New water drops slather sudzing
Parched icy droppings, bothering
To attend this dance of chance
With even a glance of grace and
God's lace is given a place to rest and
play, This sunny day.

A stream flosses,
Tossing rocks and sky droppings
Feeding tiger lilies and grass.
No loss to the tossed moss,
Clinging for its life.

Even this mountain paradise
Is awash with slices of
Natured joy, not a ploy
Of brash among the banks,
Dank from this wet place.

Ah So

By RobertEatonSokol

Happiness keeps you sweet.
Trials keep you strong
Sorrows keep you human.
Failure keeps you humble
Success keeps you glowing
But only God keeps you going.

Air Paddles Huming
By RobertEatonSokol

Round and round and no sound The
ceiling paddle fan chooses to go.

Curious, the stool gets me closer
Just missing my nose, so it throws the blow

I'm just begging for some relief
From this dead air, so close to me. Am I deaf?

The heat is not kind to those whose life
Takes youth, it's not couth, but curious to those furious.

These paddles chance their tails
And remind me that we sometimes fail to empty the pail.

This old bum gets be lost sometimes
As it hums, going round and round to the sound of?

It can take you up and
Send you back down when little else scuffs your duff does.

All Mine, This Paint Brush
By RobertEatonSokol

Stillness lies in morning dew, I knew
The night sent it with clues, its dew.
Sunlight glitters through sleepy eyes.
Through the sky and the sight of night, with all its

might Awakened by my feline's cries and no more lies,

I stretch these stiff bones as if to say by-by to sleep,
While inhaling slept on mist from cologne and brewing
The thought of coffee, softly fills my head,
Giving me the best reasons to flee my bed

A certain magic's in the air as I spy the stairs.
Ah, but not before the brush snares this hair.
The dew lies fresh on deep green grass
And sparkles like bits of broken glass.

Not a sound does nature make
In this quiet morn, adorned with
Such calm, to me, but this, I'll take
Before the world forsakes and goes fast
Beneath my feet to the street.
But not today, OK?
It's mine to keep neat on this sheet.

All Yours, This Birthday

October 27, 2018
By RobertEatonSokol

Stillness lies in morning dew, I knew
The night sent it with clues, it's dew.
Sunlight glitters through sleepy eyes.
Through the sky and the sight of night, with all its might.

Awakened by footsteps above
And your love that don't lie,
I stretch these stiff bones as if to
say, ' Bye-bye," to sleep,
While inhaling slept-on-mist from deep scents
And the brewing thought of coffee,
Softly filling my head,
Giving me the best reasons to flee my bed, instead.

A certain magic's in the air as I spy the stairs.
Ah, but not before the brush snares this one hair.
The dew lies fresh on deep green grass
And sparkles like bits of broken glass.
Not a sound does nature make in this quiet morn, Adorned with such calm for me.
But this, I'll take
Before the world forsakes and goes
fast Beneath my feet to the street. But
not today, OK?
It's your Birth Day to keep.

Already Imagined
By RobertEatonSokol

When she left, I wanted to sigh,
But instead said," my, my, my!"
While still in my bed.

As I had stacks of poems
I plucked lilacs, watered them,
Beside my bed.

With every poem I spared,
Before I went to bed, and said,
'It's been the only thought in her head."

My heart still resides in my chest,
For since she left the best of me
All I wanted to do is sigh, "but, I'm not

dead." But inside,

I was ready for these bed
posts, Ahead of me.
I had to ask myself, "What will keep her for me?"

Kissing her good-by is not my idea of being
led Back to bed but
It did cross my head, instead.

Maybe, "I Love You," would work better,
"She said," as my door closed on the lead in my foot.
And I said, "ouch," as I laid back on my couch.

Anticipation:
My Heart is Burning, Churning
By RobertEatonSokol

H	Heart of mine
E	Enter into a place, this space of mine.
A	Anointed with caring and appointed as my heart
R	Rising above, from choices to change.
T	The beginning, with joy in mind, Is my anticipation of vacation from starvation
B	Below here, where I thought I saw you,
U	Utterly enraptured with love, captured. I

R Reached into my soul, past my heart, into a **N**
Never-Never band of joy. Then you entered
I Into my world. Sharing Joy is infectious. It is **N**
Never too late to
GGive the best part of my churning, burning love.

Appreciation
By RobertEatonSokol

Working hard,
Drawing away,
He's a lovely man at bae,
I heard her say.

A gentle breeze, smiled in
passing, This lassie paid
The sweetest payment
A man could ever find or hear.

Roses not required, she's retired.
All she wants is your survey,
A tone of respect, the prospect
Of kindness from a heartfelt smile,
For a while. So, dial me up buttercup.
Sup with me. And dine away this pining day?

Arrogance
By RobertEatonSokol

Arrogance
Can be shown
In a most innocent act alone
And then blown to atonement.

When I assume you
Need my deed of assistance,
My seed of self-importance
Leads with need and
Creates embarrassment without
Your endorsement.

Autumn is Here

By RobertEatonSokol

I miss you most of all
When Autumn leaves
Start to fall, telling tall stories of
All the colors of other mothers
Sliding down these tall maple and old Oak trees
With other blokes who have no jokes to humor me with.

Musical slopes gobble
Breezes of these colorful tokens of Spring's
past With blasts of laughing gas as we delight
in spite of growing old, boldly.
Know the season is here,
To be clear, when rainbows of rich colors appear.
Magically or tragically they are going home to warm the
earth from where they birth new seeds of these wondrous
trees. As mighty trees they birth
Once more and tell new stories of lore,
More for children's delight and glee to see
The best that God has done you and me,
Under the sun to see for ever more.

Being in Love with Me

LOVE: Daring, Caring, Listening, Hearing with Respect and Acknowledgment, Seeing all Creation, Not the Parts, Alone, Matures Through Self Respect and Trust of Soul.

By RobertEatonSokol

From above,
I was given my love,
For thee and me.
But it is me I must love
So, it can give my Love to Thee.

Love of self grows
Through actions, not reactions that help
Me grow, though It is a state of mind in kind,
That helps me lengthen strengths,
Accept and shorten our weaknesses.

When we act in ways to expand
Love of self, then we are no longer above or
below Our fellow man
And can accept our soul and humble heart
With the gift of grace, and Have no need
to explain away
Our short comings where greed
And other vile of sin live.
Finding compassion for ourselves as human beings is
discovering meaning in our life where we struggle to find our
life's purpose and value. Here, we create the expectations for
living the fulfillment through our humble efforts, in life's court.

Seven Steps:
1. Become mindful.
2. Act on what you need rather than what you want.
3. Practice good self-care and basic needs
4. Set boundaries; say, No," and mean it or "YES," and cleave to it.
5. Protect yourself; chose better friends.
6. Forgive yourself
7. Live intentionally, purposefully and by design.

Blindness: Keeping it Real.
By RoberteatonSokol

What I saw, within my heart,
Was the past that was hiding, the best of me.

It was my soul, not yet bold,
The mole was hiding for my eyes to see.

What I felt was my love,
For me, waiting for Thee to be me.

What I thought, was not yet ready
For me, as I was not steady enough,
To see me.

It was a test of time to own
As I was not ready for home, alone.

The thoughts I heard, so very long ago,
Were empty words, waiting for a home
And a heart to grow, so I'd not be so low.

Today, I glow, knowing that
My heart found tenderizing, to sew.

To say, I'm no longer blind, deaf and dumb,
Can't hide the love of where I'm from.

I found humility from confusion and
delusions, Not seclusion from my love of me.

I'm real.

Breakfast and So On...

By RobertEatonSokol

Before my morning fruit blend
Sends me to my awakening;
I get up and quietly quake
To my sink to drink my gill of pills.
Next comes my whiskers and cream to quiet
Smooth dreams of soothing face smells.
Once I've satisfied all the directions of stubby quills
I spill some puny water over my lacy face dwelling this way
or that too, and…
Make way to a shower for an hour before I sour.
As I bury my sleek skin in the bin of soap;
I elope into dreams of less grandeur, to be sure.
As I complete my rapture of morning delight,
I am reminded that others wait for their turn to burn at first light.

Next to the kitchen, where the frig awaits, my studied glancing gaze. Perhaps the hazing fog lingers outside the window; then Plucking apples, blue berries, straw berries and cherries, garnished with sun ripened raisins and grapes; they find their way to the blender where they are sent to a battering tizzie, after being anointed with more juice, the ilk of cow and a bit of chocolate and utter's butter. Mother will utter the other wow! Breakfast this morning goes down with a straw for good measure.

Butterflys and Loose Skies
By RobertEatonSokol

Like a butterfly,
I saw her under the Autumn sky and,
Like my butterfly, she's beautiful, though not
mine. And as Autumn leaves the lit sky full of
Many colors and wondrous things,
She shed her wings, so I am not smothered
By mere thoughts of her fluttering,
Through my mind's eye and this wondrous sky.
All I dream of you and butterfly is the evening sky.
 It's you, not good-by.

Close Your Eyes

By RobertEatonSokol

Close your eyes,
See no lies
Close your eyes.

See me there,
When I dare to care
See me there

Send me there,
Kiss my lips.
Show me where.

You'll go where
My love compares
Cause your there. Love's not spared.

Close your eyes
Music play
All day.

Come Pray with Me
By RobertEatonSokol

Keep the sums of the be-good-ones,
Then throw the bums to beg,
For sleep down under.
They were the blunder,
Scattered across the floor,
Hoping to score more.

Toss fears out of the door
And gather tears of joy.
And let them snuggle for
Your smile, just for your dialing your day.
Night and darkness have fallen
Into my lap, filling the last gasp of my day.
Now I can sleep a few laps,
Tapping, tapping…

Collect the hurt that lingers
And scold them to a corner,
Then let those slide asunder.
Take a knee or two, but
Don't think about it.
Remember the things we are thankful for.
Discard the rest that dwells for more. Toss
them to the past, fore' if I die before The
morn, forlorn, at least our souls will last.

Courage

By RobertEatonSokol

Don't walk behind me,
I may not lead.

Don't walk in front of me.
I may not follow.

Just walk beside me
And be my fellow friend.

Being deeply loved by
someone Gives me strength.

Loving someone completely,
Gives us courage.

Cracked Illusion

By RobertEatonSokol

Happiness in a glass palace can be

Slathered by a stone face,

Then smacked by seclusion and

Slapped by lying, smiling lace.

Day and Night, Baby
By RobertEatonSokol

Damned confusion,
Sunlight and darkness,
Lining my mind in kind ways

Walking in darkness to sparks
Of light, I almost
Lost my sight, in spite of me.

Last I knew,
Day was night in contrary ways
Not a blight from spite.

I'm like a baby, change me and
Daylight makes my hidden
Bin look like Mom's been away all day,
Dismayed with wonder.

Disarming Farming and Dangerous Work

By RobertEatonSokol

Here, Stool sitting,
Hands pull white streams of drool;
Working fast to pass this lass teats and ass
Before she kicks me stool.

White splash
Smites the pooled
Bucket's docket.

A cow calls out
Her assisted
Orgasmic sound, abounding, bellowing.

And Saunters back
To meadows bay and her hay,
She baes at the loon's moon.

It's Chilly Outside Summer's Gone!
By RobertEatonSokol

Brown and colored leaves fall softly or
Sail wildly, even mildly
In a strong Autumn breeze,
With other seeds in need of a home.
And squirrels chatter,
Cheeks filled
With collected butter-nuts
Waiting for a better day, alone,
In their winter home.

Fathers Seeking Sunshine
By RobertEatonSokol

Fathers and sunshine are like
His child and their love all the while
Where they are his food for life.
They, father and child,
Can be greeted by a mild cloud
Or warm proud sunshine, on
Either hand, standing for the goodness they own
And are creating,
Their own meaning, learning and leaning
On the shelter of good, in life's fog, to find light.

Smile, dial up the wonder and remember to
Send'er up, up and away into the responding
yonder. Fathers, tasking this basking child, To ease
their mind and
Challenge growing in the pockets of loving
hearts. This child of God, seeks the warmth and
safety of A father's heart from the very start.
So, their love grows and flows towards the power of Light.

Fear and Discovery

By RobertEatonSokol

Fear can be an insidious poison
And a powerful defense, simultaneously.

Fear can create the most unbalanced
Half-truths based on missed cues and
Glowing defenses for happiness, askew.

Caution can create safe zones and
Secrete venom for attacking moles
And damaged souls, doling out
Fear from assumed safety where joy lives, awaiting.

For weavers of fear, security is as
Simple as canceling vulnerability and
Attacking the best in us. Then fear will prop up
the Worst in our rear view of you and fear of
discovery While it rains judgment on our plain
and Corrupts the surprise of joy with distain.

Finding Courage

By RobertEatonSokol

What keeps some folks at bay?
From courage, may be
Their fear of other's discovery
Of their truth in character, and
Not what their persona lay waiting for.
My real power is in my soul,
Before my faith and courage
and The power of prayer, every
day, So, I say, today.

Fireplace
By RobertEatonSokol

There's no fireplace
In our humble abode.
But a load of hopeful toads and cleaned up roaches
And the curtains are drawn.
It'll be dawn before long.

To keep out the thought of cold,
The TV reminds us, from its blank face,
That a roaring one
Would do more than keep out
The bold, blowing cold. It gets old.

The heat is on and it's somewhat cozy,
Even though I am home, I feel alone,
If not rosy. It's true, I'm envious too,
Of the neighbor's roaring fire.
My imagination is mesmerized
As the thoughts of those warm, cozy flames going higher.

Though the snow is gone,
Melted, without a trace,
I now need new slippers
And my own fire place
To celebrate the new mantle
I just planted behind
The TV console, to be.
Gee.

Good By, For Now.

By RobertEatonSokol

A sip of coffee, with toffee
Or spiced tea makes me want to be,
With her and not deterred by her frown.
A nonchalant nod with her bod;
And a good by kiss-thrown, to lie for,
And she'd simply too good
Or not at all, this fall.

House Broken

By RobertEatonSokol

Sticky place,
Where sweets run amuck,
Enticing bears, other stares,
And other mother's darling bums.

And angry buzz
Left behind,
The blind signs.

The hive got robbed again, Sent
packing, lacking character.

Oh well, this smells like pancakes .

I Am

I am that I am
I am in charge of my life
I am exceptional in my creator's eyes
I can do anything
I can be anything
I am God's child
I am trustworthy
I am brilliant

No one does me better than me.

I
Love
Me

I am Right Here, Before the Day
By RobertEatonSokol

I opened my eyes
And greeted the lit sky;
Said," my, my," as I pondered my way;
I stayed, laid smiling, for
moment, Then proceeded to pray,
For those at bay. l mused softly, even tenderly.

I opened my door,
To begin my day.
Making my life better, today,
I stopped for a moment
To seek atonement for any selfish thoughts
Before my say and lay complete.

Then I found faith in possibilities and understanding,
Driven by wisdom, cleaning
The windows of my mind
where Kindness found power in
Healing my soul, lest I be
Boring while soaring.

I Am There

By James Dillet Freeman

I am there.
You cannot see Me, yet I am the
light You see by.
You cannot hear Me, yet I am the
speak Through your voice.
You cannot feel me, yet I am the
power At work in your hands.
I am at work, though you do not
Understand my ways.
I am at work, though you do not
Recognize my works.
I am not strange visions. I am
not Mysteries.
Only in absolute stillness, beyond self,
Can you know Me, as I am, and?
Then but as a feeling and a
faith. Yet I am there. Yet I
hear. Yet I Answer.
When you need me, I am there.
Even if you deny Me, I am
there. Even when you feel most
alone, I Am there.
Even in your fears, I am there.
Even in your pain, I am there. I
am there when you pray and
When you do not pray.
I am in you, and you are in Me.
Only in your mind can you feel separate

From me, for only in your mind can

You separate from Me, for only in
mind Are the mists of "yours" and
"mine." Yet only with your mind, can
you know Me and experience Me.
Empty your heart of empty fears.
When you get yourself
Out of the way, I am there.
You can, of yourself, do nothing,
But I can do all.
And I am in all.
Though you may not see the good,
good Is there, for I am there.
I am there because I have to be,
because I am.
Only in Me does the world have
meaning; Only out of me does the world
go Forward.
I am the law on which the movement of
The stars and the growth of living cells
are Founded.
I am the love that is the Law's fulfilling.
I am assurance.
I am peace
I am oneness.
I am the law that you can live by.
I am the love that you can cling to.
I am your assurance.
I am your peace.
I am one with you.
I am.
Though you fail to find Me, I do fail you.
Though your faith in Me is unsure,
My faith in you never wavers, because I know you,
Because I love you.
Beloved, I am there.

This was taken to the moon by Colonel James Irwin on Apollo15 in 1971. A micro film of this remains on the moon. James Dillet Freeman is a poet, author and a Unity practitioner. It is estimated that it has been copied over 500 million times.

I Choose Life

By RobertEatonSokol

Can it be that life is such
A time, we limp on winged crutch
Clutching a glimpse of what's to be
When we are done - if we believe.

Can it be that death be
The ending parts of what
We knew and know?
The pain and sorrow will not be
A part of death - if we believe.

Can it be that when we are done
And life has left and death begun,
That what awaits is better still?
But I chose life and always will.

I Know You, Father

By RobertEatonSokol

My friend, you loved me when I did not.
You clothed my soul with kindness.
You fed my heart to God.
You fed God to my heart.
My friend, you sheltered me and gave me home,
And then you gave me tools,
To live and grow with.
I felt the warmth of your heart.
It took years in seared character building
To finally see thee in me.
You loved me so I could.
I covered myself with shields from fear,
Defended my heart with miles of lies,
And smiled a wily one.
Finally, I took my cloak of fears
and Fed them to God and Love
moved in.
Thank you for being my
father, So, I can be one.

I Wish Upon You
By RobertEatonSokol

I wish patience upon you,
When you are puzzled by life and what's
due, Coming at you out of the blue.

I wish awareness of God's truth and
The sand between your toes, so it
goes. And know the sounding ground
Will support, not desert you, When
little else does.

Divine is guidance and the
Encouragement and courage to Ask
for trust; you must arrive upon The
other side of lustful greed
And need. It is a lonesome, gnawed
bone, When you are alone.

Asking for wisdom and otherwise
Guidance is God's power to give,
Not yours nor scores of other tending to
Souls, hoping to mold brothers and
sisters. Forgive yourself and discover
Real power through humility

Not arrogance and fear.

Being open to not knowing the wisdom answers
Is power in the soul, not a hold on integrity?
Our creator is our power, every hour.

Imagination, Notion of Fancy
BY RobertEatonSokol

How high
Must I fly
In my mystical, whistful sky,
Where there are no limits
To my want
To try?

Joy and Fear

By RobertEatonSokol

Fear and Joy,
So dear to ego or heart, Lonesome
or full of nerve or verve
Rest, competing for sour power or peace.

Sewing ownership
Of seeds and growing feelings And
threats. Seeds pull at strings of
Imbalance and fear and threaten the
Best of choice, sending them
through Threatened egos,
Dear to some who live in these
Winds of weakness and retreats, from Joy.

Joy, counterintuitive to fear,
Flourishes in spite of other demotions
Of poor sight, where the bright light
of Hearts beating stronger, by choice.
It rains power, On glowering fear.
It's no accident.

Killer of the Crumbs
By RobertEatonSokol

I watch as the bread and cake crumbs fall onto
The counter top and some more to the floor.

Gory details follow the flies as they grab what they
can. The swallow follows the coffee smells and the
Executioner to these invading smurfs and their turf.

It's not fair that the sun's not here to light up this
maze As I gaze and curse the bug's mug.
I study, then aim for the
main Culprit to blame.
The fly swatter is a marvelous invention to mention.
I Spilled some coffee and it drips, drip, drip to the
floor, For more excitement, even delight. This has
been premeditated, in hopes of
This ant-eater scoring a more murderous killing.

I'm not the fan, really, scanning the horizon.
Oh well, it's done.
The coffee is still hot,
Even if I'm not.

Kiss Me
By RobertEatonSokol

Kiss me once
And I'm good to go.
Kiss me twice,
I'll not forgo but
Kiss me thrice and
I'll never let you go.
So,
Kiss me again and again
And I'll give it back.

Little and Naughty
By RobertEatonSokol

I love tasting
Dark valleys
Daringly bared and shared.

Love and God

By RobertEatonSokol

Happiness keeps me sweet, to keep.
Trials keep me strong, lifelong. Sorrows
keep me human and Failures kept me
humble, all along. Success keeps me
growing, sewing seeds. But only God
keeps me going.

Love Song to Him

By RobertEatonSokol

If you are floating on a river to anywhere,
And your mind takes you where loving souls
go, Send tender hearts.
Send blessings on winds of
Summertime wishes and wafts of love, from me.

If you see him on the road with a load of toads,
Tell him often, "I love him," and tell him to dare
To care to be me. Dare to see me and Thee. Being true
To beating hearts is a most important message, too. Give
him A shield to the evil that certainly lurks from other jerks.

Tell him to watch the winds of direction of change;
How it blows; it knows who goes there too.
Tell him to be tender, kind and to love
deeply, It is not a cost but
A ticket to wisdom fires.

If you see him,
Tell him I'm dwelling in; welling in his glory.
I am singing in a choir of,
Carriers of his love from above. I feel his soul
In my river of windy, winding roads. With his spirit,
The journey is one of joy, joy to loving souls.

Me
By RobertEatonSokol

There are days when I cannot
breathe But I will not give up on me.
And though the clouds will not let me
see, I will not give up on me.
Things get rough and though I
bleed, I will never die on me.

The rain comes down, but I will not drown.
The words cut deep but I will not weep,
My life to keep.
You demand I crawl
But I will stand tall for all to see.
My heart is scarred
But I see stars afar.
You cannot steal my dignity
'Cause, I won't ever give up on
me. My life is not for sale,
'Cause I'm too valuable, to me.

Mom Said, "Remember,

Love Shines," Sunshine of Mine.

By RobertEatonSokol

I know your smile
The way you look at me with
Love in the wind.
"How's the divine of mine, Said She?"
Fill us with dreams and wondrous beams off wonder
and Rhymes and other stories of how to be. Remember,
dear child,
"Live life with loving courage."
Divine spirit lasts long past
The moment she met me and thee.
Loving my destiny is imbedded
with Moments of loving trust.
Mothers do what they do, knowing
They are building life's reason
For trusting love, safely.
Being willing,
Is a state of mind
For change, not ego, the enemy of
Open, healthy hearts and minds
Where growth builds courage,
Not the scourge of missed busted trust.

Moon Shining

By RobertEatonSokol

The moon shines and lights my path
Owls hoot in murderous talk,
Stealthfully stalking,
As I walk.

My eyes follow a cunning sly
fox, Balking at my sight.
He whiffs and sniffs and whines at signs,
Pawing, scratching some rocks and locks of fur.
As I walk.

Mice scamper,
Rabbits thump, ears erect;
Both scram fast to last.
An owl swoops, scoops
The mouse's last blast and dilemma.
Rabbit's too fast.
As I walk.

Morning Hug, Bugging Me
By RobertEatonSokol

Cheek to cheek
We lay, baying in
Early morning glory and,
Swarming with thoughts
Mating me to you, too.
I hear deer bleating,
Birds singing,
Dating calls for
The wild in me
For thee to see.
My baby lays softly,
Breathing, fairly seething,
Her love to keep.
We fall to a soft slumber
And remember the bold holdings,
Molding memories of The night
past, to last.
Her skin,
Warm and supple,
Leads my imagination wandering,
Holding songs of wonder,
Longing to be sung. I was out of my mind, kind
of. Not supposing discovery but recovery
Of my heart's part and hungering for

A bowl of your soup for my soul.

My Heart Rate

By RobertEatonSokol

It's my heart rate,
Bating excitement
With exploding stars
And bearing my cast to last, That
belies by grin for the joy of, "Oh
Boy!" t'aint no toy to play with.
It's my heart, not a tart with a bleating beat,
Nor part of empty dresses and other messes Shining, pining to
be seen as flashing wondrous lines to pine on. Wow!

Oh, The Suckers,
By RobertEatonSokol

Sweet, sticky suckers coloring your tongue.
The music sung, "won't leave you,"
Hung among suckers, you bum!

Indulge yourself 'til you've had enough fun.
But dance and prance on high, perched 'til it's done, above such
shady, heady feelings like love, Here and above is a plumb.

Cooing eyes in my sky, gooey goody
surprises In this wrapper, straps her.
How easy to open for all to believe and not

deceive. What could go wrong with this song?

Your fantasies, for long, coming true, they're due.
Undeserved and served with verve,
Please pass the gravy and serve your nerve.

On Darkned Confusion
By RobertEatonSokol

Don't bay
At the moon
Too soon
After noon,
Before, it sets
And bets
On deleted
Darkness.

Please Repeat the Words

By RobertEatonSokol

Please repeat the words
So, I can unscramble
My dictionary of sounds,
Abounding between
You and me,
To thee, dear god.
Poetry is the whole, beautiful truth.

"John F. Kennedy, whose inaugural was the first in U.S. history to include public recitation of a poem, championed the value of poets. In an address to Amherst College, he said," I look forward to an America which will not be afraid of grace and beauty… When power leads men towards arrogance, poetry reminds him of his limitations. When power corrupts, poetry cleanses."

Poetry cleanses by telling the truth. At least good poetry does. It tells truth through an economy of words, by naming difficult and often inaccessible feelings. The late Jane Kenyon lifted up the artist's task in this way:" The poet's job is to tell the whole truth and nothing but the truth, in such a beautiful way that people cannot live without it.

Reddened Tear Drops

By RobertEatonSokol

Tear drops fall
From reddened eyes, laid.
A mother weeps for keeps.
She shook from dismay, as she lay.

Another stays and lays
Before their time,
Shot got her- gun crime time again.

Her photo stands
For all…tall girl
Old, bold you're told, too young to mold.

Friends wilt,
Looking dismayed,
Feeling guilt and silt,
Not a word said, but sad and mad.

The shock of loss
For me and all to see
Society bays and lays in wait
With blame and shame.

Remembering Fathers
By RobertEatonSokol

When fathers do what they are
Designed to do,
Their children can be amazing
Examples of integrity, honoring others
They are around.
When fathers simply show up,
They do not have to say anything,
Be told. Grace is in their presence, alone.
Theirs can be a dance of silence,
With a smile or frown to behold.
When fathers say no, but we want yes,
We learn discipline, with less.
They bless us with discernment,
In a tournament with loving
Character building and even grudging respect, to get.
There is nothing more powerful Than his words of
pride for you and
Nothing more humbling than his disapproval and
Removal of doubt for missed-deeds, no matter how
small. Life has a plate of wonder set aside for our
fathers. Sometimes heroes, and all times, Fathers help
create Our world, where caring, fairness and community
Is only trumpeted by the joy his love
Wove for us, his doves. He did not have to raise his voice
To be heard. When he said, " children are to be seen,
Not heard, he did not mean we should not talk,
He wanted us to ask questions and learn before we spoke.
That was his wisdom.
Remembering my father is the joy I chose to keep and sleep with.

As a child I watched with amazement
As my dad fixed anything and everything.
When dad's car needed to be fixed,
He took it apart and re-built it and
Then went for a walk with me and here we are for this talk.
When he came home from work, it
Was a picnic, you know.
Life and growing up was an adventure.
I also remember he was demanding of excellence
For all he and we knew for he had excellent teachers.
And when I could not be excellent, he still loved me
And I was confused. Still he encouraged me
To be greater than I ever thought I could.
My father was kind but not gentle
And when I decided I did not want to be like him, I
felt Again, confused and not at all amused. Then As
time and life happened;
I started becoming life my father, if perhaps a gentler,
But no less loving and filled with the wisdom that being
Quiet and observant finally rewarded me with.
His stern humility began to find its way into me,
also. So here I am, and I am reminded by those
Around me, that I am my father's son, and I am proud of him.
He became the later-day hero, I am growing into,
With love and humility.

So Rare
By RobertEatonSokol

If I dare to care,
Dignity will glow as
We grow and
Know the power of Love
And how to bear and care for it.
Giving can be such
An invigorating knowing,
Where appreciating our root
Defines our humility
Or civility, or not.

It is so rare
To find blind
Kindness
Riding on the side of dignity.
Here, gratitude gives us Joy andThis moment.

Somber is A Phonomenom, A Mood: A Sparrow Sailing Through Shallows.

By RobertEatonSokol

Lies and more peace?
Oh, the lies we tell ourselves
In pages stacked among the shelves
Of dreams and loves that should be,
But coated in our fantasies;
We swim in waters of turbulent seas
And float on lies to keep these.

Oh, the lies we take on.
We cry inside but flash a sinful grin.
We walk through fires to find the truth
But hide our fears in miss-spent youth.
The world seems bright as the moon goes down.
But we need our lies to stay aground.

Oh, the lies we're forced to live
To boost our souls, that we may give,
To love and laugh and be the one,
The universe depends on.
We need our dreams to hang on mighty tight
So, we can tuck our lies in at night,
To a Good night, outa sight,
Tonight.

Sometimes You Have to Ask Them to Leave, Not Too Politely.

By RobertEatonSokol

Barflies hover 'round you, buzzing.
Swiveling stools and pools of lies,
Squeaking all the way…'round words.
Birds, you'd rather not hear
As dear or deer's eyes in head lights, beaming.

Poetry is not spoken,
Literature is not even a token.
Instead, grunts, spurts and burps
From other hurts are broken.

Non-sensible demands, spilled. Streams of
dreams Hopes and sometimes dirty beams that
Scream lost hope or found scopes from other dopes
Eloping the ER or bar flies flying off tops
To find another start to bar my eyes with.

Stormy Weather, Kissing Me Softly.

By RobertEatonSokol

Walking, though not steadily,
While riding the wind
With a bit of sin, I muse
Dreaming through different ones.

Running, just not quickly,
I'm thinking, "not losing
Learned experiences be my guide
As I stride, even glide."

Praying more and less sore in my
head, I'm not dead from bed or lead. I
find less, I guess, as
Casts of blasts feed me with
Winds of change.

Seeing the ditches and glitches from messes,
Left by me, help me find more hope,
In stormy weather.
Memories continue to distribute
My days to tomorrows while,
Kissing me softly…, softly.

Sunlight and Billowy Clouds
By RobertEatonSokol

Raining rays of sunlight, hazing me with
warmth And birth of loving light,
In spite of my confusion and delusion, it
Stops to take a taste of me and mine.
Clouds seem to float, where ever I go,
Whether fast or slow, then go,
Mix or evaporate at any rate
Light or fluffy like Buffy butterflies or darkly Omnivorous,
even carnivorous as they block the sun from my buns, Rather
than run from all the fun.

And though not brittle, they break effortlessly and breathe the
breeze to you and me and
Then sneeze a bluff of stuff.
Clouds, pregnant with moist stuff are
Filled with whatever and wherever they can
as They cool souls, even molls. Then they
prevail,
No matter, they don't seem tough.
We think we are even from afar
from The distant star.
Even stars get no break from these
Over powering moisture bluffs
Stuffed from the sun's rays
On hazy days. No bluffing allowed.

The Beat Goes On---Pure Joy

By RoberteatonSokol

The beat goes on from sleeping,
Spirit and soda to keeping this beat.
The thump of this stump and my foot
Pump life into this lifeless floor's wood.
Out of the door, comes the Jazz Man
Running his fingers carefully,
Then wildly up the down Base, in this case.
Next comes the piano man's lace
With his gate, the trombone's sliding
Bracing for the Snare and bongo's home.
The Jazz Men, carry it home,
Though not alone, through
The marrow of a graceful sparrow,
The slide abides by gliding,
Weaving, nodding motion in this commotion
To a notion of silky lotion of emotion.
Can't deny this rhythm- no lie on my sleeves.
Geeze, what a breeze.
These notes leave me,
Pure Joy! No toys here.

The Divide: Let's Talk (Not Balk)
BY RobertEatonSokol

Now, in this moment in time,
We are wasting time of thine.
Let's not forget the spine
That gives us
Courage in character.
Encourage truth from a
Broth of grief or hope
Not a dope of guile for lies.
The flashpoint for growing
Past the path of fear,
So dear to some souls,
Can be the loss of courage,
The scourge of character.
Tolerance does not engage in
Understanding a divide,
Nor does it accept sliding pride.
Acceptance requires
Questioning and listening to the
Glistening truth when we are
Willing to hear what's dear.

Let's talk and listen.

The never-ending story, A salute to courage

By RobertEatonSokol

If you have to ask,
You'll never bask in this glory.
You'd be lacking courage
To act on your heart's
Imagination for receiving God's love.
The world's not scary because
Of those who do evil,
But from those who do nothing about it.

Smiling and hugging someone Brings
me, bowing to embrace love And
conquer my defenses. Infect Your
heart with, "Remembering why." The
birth of courage is the doing,
Not asking why. A humble, but knowing
spirit, Shouts it out, quietly, even meekly.

So, Shout!

The Storm (Is Here) Arrived

The storm is here,
It's arrived.
Battened hatched will survive.
Holding on to the cross,
I know there will be loss.
This boss tosses
Even the moss,
The cost
Of not holding on.

Wind's braying,
Sounding off through trees and seas are
plundered. Roads and toads,
Bent grass and other weeds surrender.
The offensive assaults vows and wows,
Shaped and snapped evidence of
tumult As it assaults onlookers and
Other observers of
Stormy eyes blinding, sighs, not minding.

Only mice survive and
Rats thrive on left over's and scorpions.

There Is No Limit To God's Love
By RobertEatonSokol

Being an angel for peace
Requires an aggressive stand
Against fear, warring hearts,
And other heated seeds of conflict,
To blend and mend them.

Taking a stand against the divisiveness
Of your own lying eyes, requires
Firm character to lift up love and joy
To the pinnacle of peaceful living,
And giving.

Being willing to challenge
What we think we see and,
Then be the truth before the lies that be.
Invite others to the different language
Of Love and Patience, daring to care
For the gift of Spirit, searing your souls.

The opportunities that forgiveness brings to Joy are
Joy to the worlds of children.
The power of giving selflessly
Has no ceiling, capped by our Creator
because There is no limit to God's Love. It's
the sky and that ain't no lie.

This Slippery Slope
By RobertEatonSokol

The bold responsibility of
Slippery slope riding
Never accounts for the sadness, mounting.
Smiling guile and style greets
The gates of hell in the bowels of that mountain.

You may be having a ball,
When you're slipp'in and dipp'in
Out the door for more
Sores and bruises from lice and
bumps Of loss of trusting lust.

No matter who slips and falls,
The Bells toll and calls for all
The cheap excitement and
Doesn't guarantee a long-term blast!
It doesn't last without love's cast!

For love to get past and last
It takes more
Than sass to best the lies that fly past.
The mast of this ship
Won't last, without the wind of truth and heart.

This Time, It's Sublime

By RobertEatonSokol

Standing, watching
From afar.

He sees a star,
Shining the glories of
Lantern's lites.

She sees all our dining
Built on "is," not what
Might be,
From me to see.

Time Stands For No One

By RobertEatonSokol

Standing with you,
Watching the star
It's you I see from afar.

You are what I be and see
It is you I listen to.
 Your glow and my eyes twinkle
a wrinkle.

If I could ask time to stand still
I would want to see you
Shine one more time.

Took Me From Down Seed
By RobertEatonSokol

The winds of love
Came,
Blew me away
From down
To grown up.
Seeds are rare so bare.

Toy Store and More Suckers·

By RobertEatonSokol

Looking old, though not,
Odd and holding forget-me-nots
She sits near the Carrousel, sucking a beer.
She's feeling bold. Oh well, please tell.

Little boy sees a toy 'lectric train
Wobbling across the track on
Its way back. A little girl
Begs Mom, "a quarter for the 'lectric pony."

No time for her shows,
She holds quaffed, streaked hair in her hands, Waiting
for her love to land and stand by, amid Promises He
made while standing, playing the band.

Little boy gleefully jumps, urging the
Train to follow his directions. Mommy plugs
The tender into the receiver and the girl and pony Become
one gleeful legend to remember.

Round and round the tracks go
And the train slows to a stop, while0
The little girl urges the pony to go
Faster as it also slows to stop.

The old lady, feeling
Thoughts spinning in her head dealing
With miss-spent youth.
She climbs on the Carousal and wishes
Up and down the silver pole.

And round and round the music goes.
Though wondering
What she could have said instead,
Waiting for her love to show.

Another minute, maybe two.

For a better view,
She lets go of the silver pole and dismounts,
Bends down to tie her shoe and
Smoothes wrinkles in her wool skirt, wishing
Memories wouldn't hurt, as she burps.

The lone, lost rider soon dismounts
As the lights dim, she wonders about him.
And the boy, little girl and Mom all leave
Still believing in something.

Wandering Home at Night was Tight.
There was the Play to Light my Way. Childlike fun.

By RobertEatonSokol

I wandered home in the warm rain light tonight and
Thought it was all right and outa sight. Thought I'd
leave my truck outa the muck;
And the side of the road seemed just right, tonight.
It seemed the warm night would keep the moist air
just For my failing sight and with all my might went I.
I trudged along this splendid adventure, the warm rain,
Fairly ripples, almost falling with lacy grace, then splashes by
my naked feet on this street.
Carrying my shoes seemed almost silly for this old fillie. But the swarm of warm rain drops found my smiling lips and teased my attention.
I fairly dash my gate and move with ease in these bare feet, to tease my delight, in spite of my dampened nose. My spirit goes to my clothes 'because it knows.
Occasionally, childlike fun dashes the splashes
away, Late in my day.
The day got lost, by choice, with my wet nose
Leading the way, swaying this way and that.
CHILD'S PLAY on this day!

What's Here, This Time?
It's Your Mirror.

By RoberteatonSokol

It's our lives,
As we strive
To drive confusion and
Delusions of ego
And loss of control,
No troll on your soul.

How do you,
Just to be sure,
Hear what is really said?
Listen to the mirror's message,
As different from mine,
Though sublime.

What Poetry Does For and to Me
By Robert Eaton Sokol

I find it interesting that in the language of writing- reduction, brevity and complete thought is the key to all communication. Then, does the reader or listener really hear the intended words?

Flowers scented and kitchens unvented, honors the smells and the nose knows.

A poet's job is to salute the mind by creating imagery through the senses; the nose, ears, sight, touch and taste, creating memories of moments past and views of the present. It is this task, recounting scenes for our senses and experiences without doubt and in as few words as possible that accurately describe the experience and or view of life.

A novelist tells a story that creates a new experience with great detail.

A story teller recounts an abbreviated or edited version of the novel.

The essayist's view is more a picture of the story.
The poet must "reduce," the story to the fewest possible words, yet tell the truth, while telling a glorious story through our sensory profile.

About the Author

Robert Eaton Sokol is a true Renaissance man. Heart Poet, wood sculptor, and Award-Winning new home and renovation designer. He blends his passion for life and people in everything he does. This second addition collection of poetry and prose is a sample of the bounty and journey of self-discovery. It is dedicated to all those who chose to," Celebrate Life," and all its riches.

Peace and Blessings,

Robert Eaton Sokol

www.ingramcontent.com/pod-product-compliance
Lightning Source LLC
Chambersburg PA
CBHW030532080526
44586CB00011B/407